Miffy Loves
New York City!

NYC & COMPANY
www.nycvisit.com

**Big Tent Entertainment
New York**

"Dear Grandma and Grandpa Bunny,

It's Miffy writing you a letter from New York City.
We arrived safely and I am ready to have fun!

More than 8 million people live in New York City. And,
there are so many taxis and tall buildings here!"

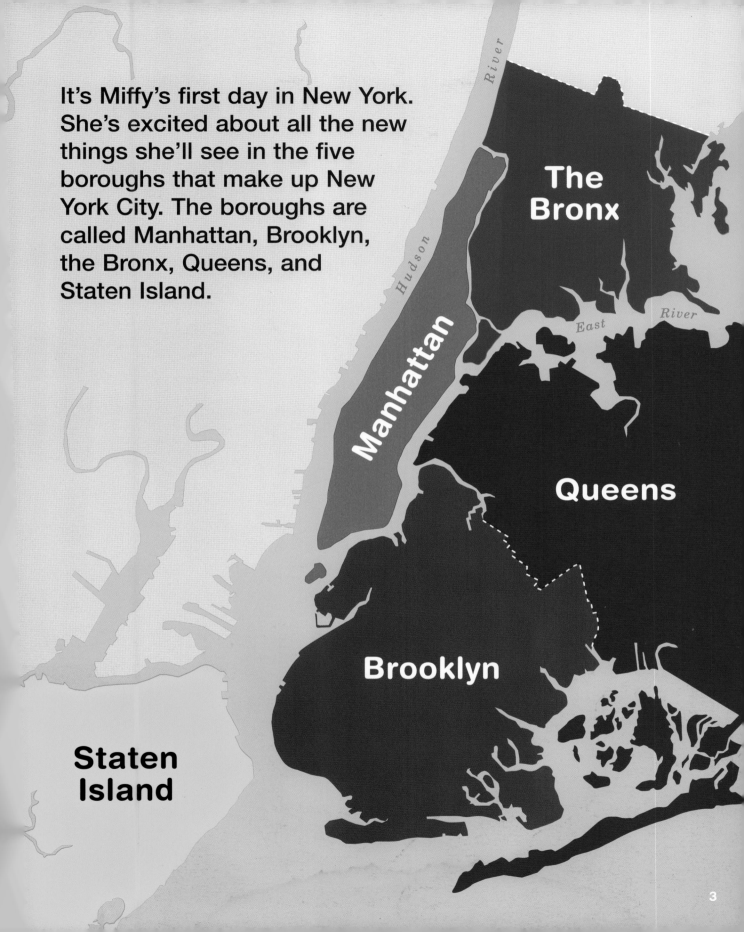

It's Miffy's first day in New York. She's excited about all the new things she'll see in the five boroughs that make up New York City. The boroughs are called Manhattan, Brooklyn, the Bronx, Queens, and Staten Island.

Hudson River

The Bronx

Manhattan

East River

Queens

Brooklyn

Staten Island

3

Miffy will start learning about New York City
by visiting the Statue of Liberty and Ellis Island.

France gave the Statue of Liberty to the United
States as a symbol of friendship. The statue
weighs an amazing 225 tons!

MISS ELLIS ISLAND

Miffy loved the museum on Ellis Island, because she saw pictures of people who came to New York from all over the world.

You can trace your family heritage on a computer if you have an ancestor that moved to America.

"Mmmm, a pretzel makes a nice snack while sightseeing!"

"Thank you, sir," Miffy says to the doorman at the hotel. "We've had a very busy day! We're going to relax in the park before dinner."

"Oh, my, this is a very big park," exclaimed Miffy. "Did you know that it took nineteen years to build Central Park and make it look the way we see it today?" asked Father Bunny.

Miffy poses for a picture on Bow Bridge in Central Park.
It's a perfect day for a walk around the park.

The Empire State Building is the tallest building in New York City, and you can go all the way up to the 102nd floor!

"Look! I can see Central Park," shouts Miffy from the observation deck on the 86th floor.

Every night the lights on the top of the Empire State Building represent something special. Miffy and her family saw red, white and blue lights because they were visiting during the July 4th holiday—it was Independence Day! Because of the celebration, they also saw a special fireworks display.

The next day Miffy rode the subway to midtown Manhattan. The subway is the fastest way to get around the city!

New York is also a great walking city. After visiting Times Square, Miffy walked to Bryant Park where a surprise awaited her.

A carousel! Miffy rode a beautifully painted horse while Mother and Father cheered her on.

Located behind the New York Public Library, Bryant Park is midtown's only large green space. It's a haven in the summertime.

Strolling further uptown, Miffy discovered the statue of Prometheus in Rockefeller Plaza.

"Look, Miffy. This is where the Christmas tree stands every December," explains Mother Bunny.

Miffy ends her day by enjoying one of her favorite paintings—*Starry Night.*

"Very beautiful," Miffy sighs. "Now, it's time to go home."

Sleep tight, Miffy.
Tomorrow will be another busy day....

Did someone say busy? Grand Central Station is one of the busiest places in New York! Hundreds of trains carry people in and out of the city. Today Miffy is catching a train to the Bronx.

"There are so many fun things to do in the Bronx," says Miffy. "What will we do today, Father?" "Our first stop is The New York Botanical Garden," Father replies. There are 250 acres to explore, but Miffy doesn't have all day, because…

...she's also going to "the house that Babe Ruth built."
Yes, the New York Yankees are playing today and it's
Miffy's first baseball game!

It's back to the Bronx for another treat—the zoo! In the Bronx Zoo, Miffy loves the "Children's Zoo" and "Jungle World." She also likes to watch the turtles,

the giraffes...

...and the elephants.

Miffy and her parents love to walk and explore.
Today they're crossing the Brooklyn Bridge—on foot!
It takes about a half hour to walk from
Manhattan to Brooklyn.

Time for a cool drink.
Next stop—Coney Island!

"That was fun! Miffy shouts after getting off the Ferris wheel at Coney Island. "Can we do that again?"

There are so many ways to get around in New York.
One of Miffy's favorites is the Staten Island ferry.
Did you know that the ferry ride is free?

Miffy has had a fun time in New York City. It's time to go home, but she has seen and learned so many things! On her last day, Miffy enjoys a bicycle ride in Corona Park in Queens. She is amazed at the size of the Unisphere, which was built in 1964 for the World's Fair.

Miffy had a wonderful vacation in New York. Here are some of the other places she visited. What is your favorite New York spot?

Enjoying a snack on the sidewalk.

Serendipity 3 is famous for their tasty frozen hot chocolate.

The marble lions in front of The New York Public Library.

Playing on the beach at Coney Island.

The City of New York

New York City as it exists today was created in 1898 when, under state charter, the city was expanded from its original confines of Manhattan to incorporate Brooklyn, Queens, the Bronx and Staten Island.

Brooklyn, situated on the southwest tip of Long Island, is today the most populous of the five boroughs. Queens to the northeast of Brooklyn, is the largest and fastest growing. The Bronx is the only borough that is part of the mainland and forms the gateway from the city to the affluent suburbs to the north. Although it remains the least populated borough, Staten Island has been growing since the completion of the Verrazano-Narrows Bridge from Brooklyn in 1964. Manhattan, the smallest borough, constitutes the heart of the city.

Lay of the Land

Although New York has an excellent mass transit system, you'll spend much of your time walking the streets. Manhattan's streets are laid out in a grid pattern. Streets run east-west and avenues run north-south. Fifth Avenue is the dividing line between east and west addresses. Generally, even-numbered streets are eastbound; odd-numbered streets are westbound. In lower Manhattan (below 14th Street) most streets have names rather than numbers.

Downtown is south; uptown, north. "Downtown" also refers to the area below 14th Street. Midtown stretches roughly from 34th Street to 59th Street; Uptown is the area north of that.

New York City Essentials

Emergency: Dial 911.
All other New York City services: Dial 311.
Area Codes: Area codes must now be used for every call in New York City. Dial 1 + area code + seven-digit number.
Manhattan: 212, 646, 917.
Bronx, Brooklyn, Queens, Staten Island: 347, 718, 917.

Planning Your Trip

Before you go, contact NYC & Company, New York City's official tourism marketing organization for information and special offers on sightseeing, accommodations, travel packages, recreation opportunities and special events.

NYC's Official Visitor Information Center: 810 Seventh Ave. between 52nd & 53rd Sts., 212-484-1222; www.nycvisit.com Open: Mon-Fri 8:30am-6pm, Sat, Sun & holidays 9am-5pm. Thanksgiving Day, Christmas Day and New Year's Day 9am-3pm. Subway: B, D or E train to 7th Ave. (and 53rd St.); N, R, S or Q to 57th St.; or 1, 9 to 50th St. New York City's Official Visitor Information Center is the city's official source for information on everything there is to do and see in New York City including hotels, culture, dining, shopping, sightseeing, events, attractions, tours, and transportation. The Center features free brochures, discount coupons to attractions and theaters, multilingual visitor information counselors, ATM and MetroCard vending machine. Stop in, pick up brochures and discount coupons, find out what's going on, get directions… it's a great place to start your visit.

City Hall Park Visitor Information Kiosk: Southern tip of City Hall Park on the Broadway sidewalk at Park Row. Open: Mon-Fri 9am to 6pm; Sat, Sun & holidays 10am-6pm. Subway: 1, 2 to Park Place; N, R, 4, 5 or 6 to Brooklyn Bridge/City Hall; A, C to Broadway/Nassau St; E to Chambers; or the J, M, Z to Fulton St.

Harlem Visitor Information Kiosk: Adam Clayton Powell State Office Building Plaza, 163 West 125th St. and Adam Clayton Powell, Jr. Boulevard (Seventh Ave.) Open: Mon-Fri 9am-6pm; Sat-Sun 10am-6pm. Subway: A, B, C, D or 2, 3 to 125th St.

NYC Online: In addition to the official Big Apple site, other companies run Web sites chock-full of visitor information and useful links. Here is a sampling of places where you can find answers to your questions:
http://gonyc.about.com
www.cityguidemagazine.com
www.newyork.citysearch.com
www.ny.com
http://citypass.net
www.in-newyork.com
www.newyorkmetro.com
www.timessquarebid.org

Public Transportation

The Metropolitan Transportation Authority (MTA) oversees an extensive network of subways, buses and commuter trains throughout the area. The MTA's Travel Information Center (718-330-1234; www.mta.nyc.ny.us/nyct) provides route and fare information for all subway and bus lines. System maps and timetables are available on buses, in subway stations, at visitor centers and at hotels.

Subway: The subway is the most efficient way to navigate the city. Virtually all lines run 24hrs/day, with the time between trains ranging from every 2–5 minutes during rush hours to every 20–30 minutes between midnight and 5am. Travelers must purchase a MetroCard either at a ticket booth or at a vending machine to ride. The base fare is $2. When riding the subway late at night, try to ride in the car carrying the train's conductor (usually at the front of the train).

City Buses: New York City Transit buses generally operate daily 5:30am–2am. Some routes on major corridors run 24hrs/day. Route maps are posted at bus stops and in back of the driver's seat on buses; ask if you're unsure. Rides cost $2 and can be deducted from a MetroCard or paid with exact change.

Taxis: www.nyc.gov/html/tlc. Only yellow taxi cabs with roof medallions showing the taxi number are authorized by the city's Taxi and Limousine Commission to pick up passengers on the street (empty taxis have their numbers illuminated). Rate schedule: $2 for the first 1/5 mile, 30¢ for each additional 1/5 mile, and 20¢ per minute of waiting time.

New York City Attractions

These are the sites Miffy and her family visited in this book.

Brooklyn Bridge page 24
From the Manhattan side: The pedestrian walkway can be reached by crossing Park Row from City Hall Park, or from the Brooklyn Bridge-City Hall subway station. From the Brooklyn side: Access the walkway from the High St.-Brooklyn Bridge subway station. Subway: in Manhattan: 6 to Brooklyn Bridge-City Hall; in Brooklyn: A, C to High-Brooklyn Bridge.

Bronx Zoo page 23
Bronx River Pkwy. at Fordham Rd., 718-367-1010; www.bronx-zoo.com. Admission: free for children under 2, $6 children, $11 adults. Open: Apr-Oct Mon-Fri 10am-5pm, weekends and holidays 10am-5:30pm; rest of year daily 10am-4:30pm. Subway: 2 to Pelham Parkway to reach Bronx Parkway entrance to the zoo

Bryant Park Carousel page 15
6th Ave. between West 40th and 42nd Sts. Fare: $1.50. Open: daily. Subway: B, D, F, N to 42nd St. or 7 to 5th Ave.

Central Park pages 9-11
From 59th St. to 110th St.; 5th Ave. to Central Park West. Admission: free. Open: daily. Subway: B, C to 59th, 72nd, 81st, 86th, 96th and 103rd Sts. on the west side of the park. Or, A, C, D, 1, 9 to 59th St.-Columbus Circle.

Coney Island page 25 and page 29
South Brooklyn. Subway: F, Q to West 8th St.-NY Aquarium in Brooklyn.

Ellis Island Immigration Museum page 6
In New York Harbor, 212-363-3200; www.ellisisland.org. Admission: free. Open: daily 9am-5pm; closed December 25. See "Statue of Liberty" below for ferry information. Subway: 4, 5 to Bowling Green or 1, 9 to South Ferry.

Empire State Building pages 12-13
350 5th Ave., 212-736-3100; www.esbnyc.com. Admission: free for children under 5, $6 children 5-11, $11 adults. Open: daily 9:30am—midnight. Subway: B, D, F, N, Q, R to 34th St.

Grand Central Station page 19
42nd St. at Park Ave. Subway: 4, 5, 6, 7 to Grand Central-42nd St.

The New York Botanical Garden page 20
200 St. and Kazimiroff Blvd. Open: Apr-Oct, Tue-Sun 10am-6pm. Rest of year: Tue-Sun 10am-4pm. Closed Thanksgiving Day and December 25. Subway: D, 4 to Bedford Park Blvd., walk east to Garden Gate. Or, take Metro North from Grand Central Station to Botanical Garden Station.

New York Public Library page 29
476 5th Ave. (between West 40th and 42nd Sts.), 212-930-0830; www.nypl.org. Open: year-round Tue-Wed 11am-7:30pm, Thu-Sat 11am-6pm; closed major holidays. One-hour guided tours available Mon-Sat 11am and 2pm. Subway: B, D, F, N to 42nd St. or 7 to 5th Ave.

The Plaza page 8
5th Ave. at Central Park South, 212-759-3000 or 800-759-3000; www.fairmont.com. Subway: N, R, W to 5th Ave.

Rockefeller Plaza page 16
Rockefeller Plaza is situated within the Rockefeller Center complex of buildings located between 5th and 7th Avenues and 47th and 52nd Streets. Subway: B, D, F to 47-50 Sts.-Rockefeller Center.

Roosevelt Island Tram page 26
Second Avenue and 60th St.; www.rioc.com. Fare: $1.50. Subway: 4, 5, 6 to 59th St.

Serendipity 3 page 29
225 E. 60th St. (between 2nd and 3rd Aves.), 212-838-3531. Subway: 4, 5, 6 to 59th St.

Staten Island Ferry page 26
Battery Park. No charge. Subway: N, R to Whitehall St. or 1, 9 to South Ferry.

Statue of Liberty page 5
On Liberty Island in New York Harbor. Fare: free for Liberty Island. $3 children 3-17, $8 adults for round-trip ferry ride to both the Statue of Liberty and Ellis Island. The ticket office is located at Castle Clinton National Monument. Ferries depart Battery Park South in Manhattan July-Aug daily 8:30am-4:30pm every 30 minutes. Rest of year daily 9am-3:30pm every 45 minutes. No service December 25. Subway: 4, 5 to Bowling Green or 1, 9 to South Ferry.

Unisphere page 28
In Flushing Meadows-Corona Park. Subway: 7 to Willets Point-Shea Stadium.

Yankee Stadium page 21
River Ave. and E. 161st St. in the Bronx, 718-579-4531; www.yankees.com. Subway: 4, B, D to 161st St.

Other New York Attractions for Young Children

American Museum of Natural History
Central Park West at 79th St., 212-769-5100; www.amnh.org. Admission: free for children under 2, $6 children 2-12, $7.50 students, $10 adults. Open: daily 10am-5:45pm; closed Thanksgiving Day and December 25. Subway: B, C to 81st St. or 1, 9 to 79th St.

Brooklyn Children's Museum
145 Brooklyn Ave. (at St. Mark's Ave.), 718-735-4400; www.brooklynkids.org. Admission: $4 per person. Open: Wed-Fri 2-5pm, Sat-Sun 10am-5pm; July-Aug Mon and Wed-Thurs noon-5pm; Fri noon-6:30pm, Sat-Sun 10am-5pm. Subway: 3 to Kingston Ave., walk 6 blocks on Kingston Avenue to St. Mark's Avenue, and turn left.

Central Park Wildlife Center and Tisch Children's Zoo
In Central Park near the entrance at 5th Ave. and 64th St., 212-861-6030. Admission: free for children under 2, $.50 children 3-12, $3.50 adults. Open: Nov-Mar daily 10am-4:30pm; Apr-Oct Mon-Fri 10am-5pm, Sat-Sun 10am-5:30pm. Subway: N, R to 5th Ave.

Children's Museum of Manhattan
212 W. 83rd St. (between Broadway and Amsterdam Ave.), 212-721-1234; www.cmom.org. Admission: free for children under 1, $6 children and adults. Open: Wed-Sun 10am—5pm. Subway: 1, 9 to 79th St. or B, C to 81st St.

South Street Seaport
12 Fulton St. (between Water and South Sts.), 212-748-8600; www.southstseaport.com. Admission is free to the historic district, its shops, restaurants, piers and Fulton Market. $3 children, $4 students, $6 adults for admission to the gallery, historic ships, special programs, guided tours. Purchase tickets at the visitor center located at 12-14 Fulton St. Open: Apr-Sept daily 10am-6pm (until 8pm on Thurs), rest of year Wed-Mon 10am-5pm. Closed January 1, Thanksgiving Day, and December 25. Subway: 2, 3, 4 to Fulton St. or A, C to Broadway-Nassau.

Times Square
42nd St. at 7th Ave./Broadway. Subway: 1, 2, 3, 7, 9, N, Q, R, W to Times Square-42nd St.

(Note: All information is subject to change. Please confirm prices and hours of operation before visiting the places mentioned in this book.)

Courtesy of

Big Tent Entertainment
216 West 18th Street
New York, New York 10011

Illustrations Dick Bruna © copyright Mercis bv, 1953-2003.
Published in the U.S. in 2003 by Big Tent Entertainment, New York.
Publication licensed by Mercis Publishing bv, Amsterdam, through Big Tent Entertainment.

Photographs © copyright Cynthia Malaran: Cover image of Manhattan Bridge and page 32.
Photographs © copyright Alan "Battman" Batt: Pages 01, 08, 10-11, 12, 13b, 14, 15, 19, 23, 25, 28, 29a, 29b, 29d.
Photographs © copyright Jeff Greenberg/NYC & Company, Inc.: Pages 04, 05, 06, 07, 13a, 16, 17, 24, 26, 27, 29c.
Photographs © copyright Joseph Pobereskin/NYC & Company, Inc.: Page 09.
Photographs © copyright NYC & Company, Inc.: Pages 20, 21.
2003 Noggin LLC. Noggin and all related titles, characters and logos are trademarks of Viacom International Inc.
All rights reserved.
Map courtesy of Michelin Travel Publications
Interior and cover design: Cynthia Malaran

ISBN (HC): 1-59226-179-5
Library of Congress Control Number (HC): 2003110672
ISBN (PBK): ISBN: 1-59226-186-8
Library of Congress Control Number (PBK): Available from the Library of Congress.

Printed in Hong Kong.
All rights reserved.

10 9 8 7 6 5 4 3 2